Original title:
Watered with Love

Copyright © 2025 Creative Arts Management OÜ
All rights reserved.

Author: Atticus Thornton
ISBN HARDBACK: 978-1-80581-784-0
ISBN PAPERBACK: 978-1-80581-311-8
ISBN EBOOK: 978-1-80581-784-0

Tides of Togetherness

In the sea, we float as one,
Duck-faced splashes, what fun!
Waves tickle our silly toes,
As laughter in the currents flows.

Seagulls squawk with jealous glee,
They wish they swam like you and me!
Our boat's a dance on foamy trails,
As we spin to love's joyful wails.

Drenched in Devotion

A slip, a slide, we tumble down,
Splashing water like a crown.
Heart-shaped puddles mark our feet,
As we giggle through the heat.

Raindrops drip from open eyes,
We're puddle-splashing, what a surprise!
Umbrellas turn to boats at will,
Our love's a storm; it gives a thrill.

Nourished by the Stream

We dipped our toes in muddy bliss,
With every splash, a gentle kiss.
The fish look up with curious eyes,
"Do you love her?" one replies.

Bubbles rise as we share a smile,
The laughter flows for quite a while.
Nature's whisper, sweet and clear,
In every splash, our hearts sincere.

Parting the Water's Veil

Like mermaids lost beneath the foam,
We weave through rivers, far from home.
With every wave, our spirits soar,
As we splash like never before!

Caught in a whirlpool of delight,
Two fish dance under the starlight.
With water guns, we wage our fight,
And laugh until we're out of sight.

Drifting Leaves and Hearts

A leaf fell down with a silly grin,
It whispered jokes, it danced with the wind.
The puddles giggled, splashed at their feet,
As raindrops joined in with a tap-tap beat.

The trees held their breath in a comical cheer,
While squirrels debated who'd fly up here.
A couple of rabbits rolled over in glee,
Chasing each other, as wild as can be.

From branches above, a cat turned his head,
Confused by the laughter, he tumbled instead.
With a bounce and a flounce, he clumsily leapt,
Out of a dream, where all kittens slept.

So gather your friends, let the fun overflow,
With giggles and grins, let your spirits glow.
In nature's embrace, where playfulness glides,
We'll dance with the leaves, where joy never hides.

Reflections on a Still Pond

A frog once jumped, oh what a splash,
He thought he'd catch a lovely sash.
With all his hops, he lost his aim,
And landed plop—how very lame!

The fish just laughed, they rolled with glee,
In circles round, they danced with glee.
They whispered secrets, deep and wide,
Of how the frog just couldn't glide.

Oasis of Warmth

In the desert heat, the cactus sways,
It grumbles softly, through its days.
"More love, less sun," it might lament,
While casting shadows, much intent.

A doorbell rings, a lizard's friend,
With water bottles they descend.
They laugh and sip, a tiny whirl,
While cactus rolls, in friendship's pearl.

Hidden Currents of Care

A river flows, but don't be fooled,
It tells a tale of love unspooled.
With every bend, it giggles loud,
As fish parade, they form a crowd.

A turtle naps, caught in the waves,
Dreaming of treasure, and hidden caves.
"Just a nibble!" shouts a bass,
As food floats by like first-class grass.

Melodies of Mist

In the morning fog, a chorus sings,
With water droplets plucking strings.
A breeze comes through, a cheeky tease,
Rustling leaves, it shakes the trees.

A squirrel dances, spry and spry,
In misty realms, he winks an eye.
He spins around, a dizzy whirl,
As laughter echoes, a joyful twirl.

Edges of a Liquid Heart

In the pond of my dreams, I slipped and fell,
Kissing the ducks who thought I could tell.
They quacked in delight, and I splashed with glee,
Turns out, I'm the star of a wet comedy!

Thought I'd write you a note on a lily pad,
But it floated away; oh, wasn't that rad?
My love floats like bubbles, so frothy and light,
Though it pops with a giggle, it feels just right.

Streams of Passion in Moonlight

In the twilight, two fish began to dance,
Wiggling and giggling, gave love a chance.
Splashing around as the moon gave a wink,
Plump little goldfish on the edge of the sink!

They swirled in the current, trying out moves,
Bumping their fins, oh, they were such grooves!
Their love was a splashy, ridiculous sight,
With a tail flick, they glimmered through the night!

Mists of Nostalgia

I wandered the fog, with a rubber duck,
Squeaking my way through memories of luck.
The mists wore a grin, as I splashed around,
Waves of old laughter in puddles I found.

With whispers of water, the past came to play,
A boat made of leaves drifted on its way.
Each droplet held stories I'd long since tucked,
And giggles returned like a friend who's unstuck.

The Overflowing Cup of Kindness

My teacup runneth over with jokes and delight,
Filled to the brim with a splash every night.
Friends gather 'round for a sip and a chuckle,
Even the teapot joins in the shuffle!

With marshmallows bouncing like thoughts in my head,
Each sip makes us goofy, break bread with the bread.
So let's pour out laughter, let's raise a good cheer,
In a cup overflowing, find love crystal clear!

Raindrops on a Velvet Soul

A cloud sneezed, and down it fell,
My heart's in puddles, can't you tell?
I splashed around, so full of glee,
Dancing in drops, just like a spree.

Umbrellas flipped, the rain's a tease,
Each drip brings laughter, if you please.
With every splash, a giggle so light,
We're all wet noodles in this delight!

So bring on the storms, the skies, the downpour,
I'll waddle and skip, I'll sing and I'll roar.
In this water ballet, we're all a bit mad,
Skipping stones with joy, it's all just so rad!

In puddles we leap, with squishy shoes,
Every raindrop wins, there's nothing to lose.
With hearts like sponges, we soak it all in,
What a wet riot, let the fun begin!

The Ocean's Embrace of Sentiment

Oh, the ocean called me for a swim,
Its waves were grinning, not a whim.
I tripped on sand, fell flat on my face,
Saltwater tickles, what a funny place!

Seagulls giggle, they steal my fries,
With each wave's laughter, right near my thighs.
Splashing around with the fish so bold,
Who knew a seaweed wig could be gold?

The tide brings treasures, but sometimes a shoe,
A floaty that's bursting, oh, who knew it flew?
With every splash, I'm singing a tune,
Under the sunshine, dancing 'til noon!

So let's ride the waves, with shouts and cheers,
Embracing the ocean, despite all our fears.
For here in the surf, we dream and we play,
In this wet wonderland, let's live for today!

Love's Fluidity in Every Drop

Bubbles bobbing, a fizzy sensation,
My heart's a drink, in sweet celebration.
I sip on the giggles, let out a cheer,
Fizzy with laughter, I'll bring you near!

Swirling around in a glass half-full,
Life's quite the party, it's never dull.
With each sip taken, the smiles grow tall,
Frothy and funny, let's have a ball!

Sprinkles of joy float on top of the scene,
Whipped cream clouds and jellybean sheen.
Take a big gulp, let the flavors collide,
In a rainbow of fun, let our hearts glide!

With straws as our lances, we joust for the thrill,
Pouring out laughter, like time has stood still.
Every drop's magic, so let's clink a toast,
To love's funny spills, we'll cherish the most!

Currents of Compassion

In rivers of giggles, we drift and slide,
With kindness as oars, we flow with pride.
Bumping our boats in a friendly race,
Look out for the ducks in a dash for first place!

We paddle with joy, launch splashes galore,
A water fight bubbling, who could ask for more?
Let's wade through the fun, with friends all about,
With laughter like ripples, we twist and shout!

The current's a tease, pulling me near,
But I stand my ground, with splashes of cheer.
From tributaries of smiles, a flood of delight,
In this river of friendship, everything's bright!

So grab your life vests, it's a splish-splash scene,
With our arms wide open, we'll keep it serene.
For currents of compassion flow strong and free,
In this aquatic adventure, you'll always have me!

Embracing the Ocean's Flow

A fish in a tux, doing the twist,
Splashes around, you can't resist.
Seagulls squawk jokes, parrot a rhyme,
Dancing with waves, it's party time!

Shells tell tales of sandcastle kings,
Seashells with crowns and seashells with rings.
A crab in a sarong, the conch joins the fun,
Under the bright, shining sun!

Mermaids giggle, pull pranks on the shore,
Hiding your sandals—what else is in store?
The tide rolls in with a chuckle so grand,
Soaking the feet of those on the sand.

A whale with a hat just breezed by,
He tipped it to dolphins—oh my oh my!
The ocean's a party, come take a dip,
With laughter and wriggles, now that's a trip!

River of Dreams

A river flows with dreams afloat,
Napping on leaves, they gently dote.
Fish play tag, bubbles pop in glee,
Paddling downstream, just you and me.

A frog wears glasses, counting the stars,
While turtles race with little toy cars.
The water sings songs, so silly and bright,
Giggling as it sparkles under moonlight.

A raft made of candy, who could resist?
Join the parade, here's a sweet twist!
Splashing through laughter, we drift along,
Where every swirl finds its own silly song.

In this river, our whims take flight,
Frogs croak jokes, oh what a sight!
Flowing with joy, though it may seem absurd,
We laugh and we love, not a word is heard!

Love Like a Gentle Rain

Pitter-patter giggles, raindrops fall,
Singing on rooftops, they play and call.
Umbrellas become boats with a splash,
As puddles form laughter, oh what a crash!

Raincoats in colors, a bright happy mess,
Jumping like frogs, we dance nonetheless.
Raindrops like confetti, float down with delight,
A shower of smiles, what a blissful sight!

A cloud's tickling whim, a playful tease,
Mist turning into jokes that float with the breeze.
A gentle drizzle, no need to frown,
Just dance in the rain, let worries drown.

Together we giggle, shivering, wet,
Making the best of each drop that we get.
With love tumbling down, like water so fine,
Life's a cheeky parade, all yours and mine!

Marshes of Remembering

In marshes thick with memories bright,
Swamp critters share tales under moonlight.
Frogs croak the stories of days gone by,
While fireflies twinkle like stars in the sky.

A heron tells puns with a serious face,
While the turtles all chuckle, slow at their pace.
Kingdoms of reeds swaying, sharing their lore,
Laughter that echoes, forever and more.

The bog is a stage, and everyone plays,
Each ripple a giggle, throughout all our days.
Water lilies wink as they spin and twirl,
In this land of remember, let laughter unfurl.

The marsh is a treasure, a playful mirth,
Where every soft splash has its own worth.
With memories alive and stories to share,
In the marshes we wander, without a care!

Spring Showers of Tenderness

Raindrops tickle flowers' cheeks,
They giggle in delight,
The sun then joins this silly game,
Winks with all its might.

Puddles dance like happy clowns,
Jumping all around,
Rubber boots make quite the splash,
In this joy we've found.

Clouds wear hats of fluffy white,
Sweaters stitched with glee,
They send a sprinkle here and there,
To wet our jubilee.

Nature's chuckle fills the air,
As breezes start to hum,
So here we are, just soaking up,
The fun that's yet to come.

Beneath the Surface

Bubbles rise like giggles fair,
Fish are laughing too,
Underneath the water's glow,
Splashes just for you.

A turtle with a silly face,
Winks at a passing snail,
They share jokes and funny tales,
In their underwater vale.

Seaweed sways to rhythms bright,
While crabs dance on the floor,
With pirate hats, they make a scene,
Who could ask for more?

Every ripple sings a tune,
Joy flows without a care,
Beneath the surface, laughter grows,
In the ocean's lair.

The Dance of Water and Heart

A fountain sprays confetti drops,
Laughter fills the square,
The water spins on tiptoes,
For love is everywhere.

Ducks are crooning silly songs,
As they waddle near,
One slipped in—oh what a splash!
A chorus made of cheer!

Rivers swirl as if they sigh,
In tango with the breeze,
Their partners leap and prance around,
With jovialities.

Every splash a joke they tell,
As bubbles float away,
In the dance of heart and flow,
They make a merry play.

Harvesting Harmony

We gather laughter like fresh rain,
In barrels big and wide,
With every drop, a memory,
Of joy we cannot hide.

Carrots dance beneath the soil,
Tomatoes blush with pride,
While peas sing tunes of harmony,
In their leafy guide.

The harvest basket's brimmed with cheer,
Fruits cheer us with their glow,
As we skip hand-in-hand with joy,
To share the love we sow.

In every bite, a chuckle sweet,
As flavors intertwine,
We feast upon the laughter brought,
In this meal divine.

Flooded with Memories

A memory jog, a splash of cheer,
The past comes rushing, never fear.
Like a tap that's on, it won't turn off,
With each new thought, I laugh and scoff.

Dancing ducks in a puddle wide,
Each quack a tale of laughter and pride.
The rain-soaked socks, the dripping hats,
Oh, the joy of soaking wet chitchats!

The misty mornings, a whimsical sight,
With coffee spills and a pillow fight.
Where pages from books dance in the stream,
Life's a splash! Or is it a dream?

In a flood of joy, we brightly float,
Chasing memories like kids with a boat.
The current of laughter keeps us afloat,
Silly moments that make us gloat.

Hummingbird and Rain

A hummingbird buzzed with a splashy dare,
While rain clouds gathered, causing quite a scare.
It hovered near flowers, sipping with glee,
Drenched in frivolity, just like me!

Raindrops became a sweet serenade,
Each drop a chuckle, a playful charade.
Splashing about in a puddle of fun,
Chasing around like a race just begun!

The bird darts quick, in a dizzying flight,
While I fumble and slip—what a comical sight!
With each gust of breeze and whimsical sway,
I laugh at the antics of this silly day!

So here's to the rain and the feathered prank,
For laughter and joy, we've got high rank!
With wings and water, we'll swirl and twirl,
Life's a giggle in this giddy whirl.

Love's Gentle Cascade

A stream of giggles flows from the heart,
Each chuckle and snicker, a splash of art.
Tiny ripples of joy skip along,
In the brook of affection, we both belong.

The gentle cascade of jokes and glee,
Turns serious moments into a spree.
In puddles of laughter, we jump and play,
Making mischief in our own sweet way!

With twinkling eyes, we share our dreams,
Like floating leaves in a gushing stream.
Sipping on smiles, we bask in this glow,
In the creek of delight, endlessly flow.

Dancing in torrents, life feels so bright,
With silly banter lighting the night.
Every splash a whisper, every wave a grin,
In love's gentle stream, we both dive in.

Liquid Lullabies

In waters so warm, we sway and twist,
Tiny splashes create a comedy mist.
Each drop a giggle, soft lullabies,
A symphony brewed beneath the skies.

With ripples of joy and tides of jest,
We sail through silliness; it's the best!
A floating raft of dreams and cheer,
Where chuckles echo, loud and clear.

The rain taps softly, like a gentle tune,
While frogs croak out a rhythm at noon.
We dance in puddles, twirling with ease,
Chasing the clouds, tickled by the breeze.

So let the water sing its song of fun,
In this flow of laughter, we're never done.
With liquid lullabies wrapping us tight,
We'll drift on joy until the night.

Nurtured by Waves

In the sea of giggles, we splash,
Bubbles tickle noses, in a dash.
Sand castles crumble with a roar,
Oh, the salty jokes we adore!

Crabs scuttle by in a funny dance,
We trade our ice cream for a chance.
To dive deep into the ocean's grin,
And find the laughter tucked within.

The Depths of Affection

I've got a fish that loves to tease,
Swims around with the greatest ease.
It winks at me with scaly delight,
And does the backstroke late at night.

Seaweed sways to a silly tune,
While jellyfish float and act like goons.
My heart floats high on bubbles of glee,
In this ocean of love, just you and me.

Gentle Ripples of Care

Paddling about in a rubber boat,
We giggle and splash, oh what a quote!
Ducklings quack in synchrony,
As we serenade them comically.

"Hold my drink!" I shout with glee,
As my friend dives in to chase a bee.
They emerge dripping with a bold flair,
Surprised at the sting, but love's everywhere!

Flowing Emotions

A river runs cool, it whispers a tune,
We skip stones and laugh, oh what a boon!
The fish are giggling, the frogs sing along,
As we invent rhymes that just feel wrong.

With every splash, our friendship grows,
Like water balloons filled up with woes.
We throw them with laughs and joyous screams,
In this playful world of wiggly dreams.

Sowing Seeds of Serenity

In pots of giggles, we plant our joy,
With sprinkle canisters, oh what a ploy!
Our weeds wear hats, they dance and sway,
While sunshine chuckles, brightens the day.

Let's water our puns, make them grow tall,
With jokes as fertilizer, we'll never stall.
The daisies smile, but the tulips pout,
Because they forgot what love's all about!

Butterflies flutter, wearing silly shoes,
While bumblebees sing the latest news.
With laughter like rain, we'll nurture each sprout,
In this garden of chuckles, there's never a doubt.

So sow your seeds with a goofy grin,
Let the happiness blossom, let the fun begin!
For in this floral kingdom, take a look and see,
That joy's the sunshine, as bright as can be.

Currents of Connection

In a river of giggles, we float along,
With fish that whistle our favorite song.
The turtles wear ties, taking their time,
While splashes of laughter create a rhyme.

The ducks are gossiping, bobbing about,
Quacking their secrets, without any doubt.
Frogs leap in rhythm, hop with a cheer,
Synchronized swimming, oh dear, oh dear!

We paddle our boats made of laughter and glee,
Navigating the rapids, just you and me.
With giggles like bubbles, we rise and we fall,
As the current of friendship carries us all.

So dip your toes in this silvery stream,
Splash joy on your friends, live your wildest dream!
For in these waters, a bond so bright,
Floats along merrily, in pure delight.

Fluid Bonds

With cups full of smiles, we toast to our crew,
To friendships that shimmer like morning dew.
Bubbles of friendship, float up and away,
In this fizzy world, let's dance and play.

Our laughter's the current, it flows and it bends,
Creating a river that never ends.
We're all silly fish in a sea made of glee,
Splashing around just to feel fancy-free.

With cups of confetti, we drink in delight,
Swirling in water, everything feels right.
Mix a pinch of humor, a dash of fun,
Together we shine like the morning sun.

So here's to the bonds that flow like a stream,
In a world full of giggles, we'll always beam!
With fluid connections, we'll never part,
For laughter and love are the best kind of art.

Streams of Compassion

With a splash of kindness, we dive right in,
Creating ripples with every little grin.
The ocean of warmth surrounds us at play,
Waves of affection wash worries away.

Our friendship's a fountain, gushing and bright,
Making rainbows sparkle in laughter's pure light.
When life throws rocks, we just laugh and shout,
Because silly times can turn any pout!

Let's build our bridges with giggles and cheer,
In a river of kindness, we've nothing to fear.
Pouring compassion like drinks at a bash,
Stirring up joy with a delightful splash.

So come take a dip in this caring stream,
Together we'll flourish, share every dream!
For in this vast ocean of giggly glee,
We find all our treasures, just you and me.

Crystals and Currents of Care

In the garden where fingers dig,
We find a frog wearing a wig.
He leaps with joy, splashing around,
Waving his hands, he's lost and found.

Dew on the grass, glistening bright,
A snail on a mission, oh what a sight!
He's in a hurry but moves so slow,
Chasing a raindrop, what a show!

Birds sing loudly, a comedic choir,
While worms dance gladly, never tire.
With every drop, they twist and twirl,
Nature's stage, it's a funny whirl!

So let's toast to the sprinkles and sprays,
Where laughter grows in the sun's warm rays.
For nature's laughter, let's not forget,
In this playful world, we're all set!

Nature's Serenade of Connection

A squirrel wearing boots, oh what a sight,
Bounces along, feeling quite light.
He offers acorns to the nearest bee,
Who buzzes back, 'Hey, look at me!'

Trees sway gently, doing a jig,
A raccoon joins in, he's such a big.
With twirls and spins, they call out loud,
Sunshine smiles, they're a merry crowd.

The brook giggles, bubbling with cheer,
Inviting frogs to hop over here.
'Come join the party, bring your best snack,
Together we'll dance, no need to look back!'

As fireflies spark, lighting the night,
We'll laugh and chuckle, what a delight!
In this crazy world of joy and cheer,
Nature sings softly, simply sincere.

The Deep Well of Affection

In the garden of puddles, we frolic and play,
A goldfish named Gerald steals all the sway.
He juggles with raindrops, careful and spry,
While the frogs cheer him on, oh my, oh my!

A turtle named Ted brings a bar of soap,
He slides on his shell and gives a great hop.
He sings out a tune, so silly, so sweet,
In this bath full of giggles, we dance to the beat.

With watering cans full of silly old pranks,
The daisies all chuckle and join in the ranks.
Butterflies flutter with laughter and grace,
In this whimsical well, love sprinkles the space.

When clouds start to giggle, raining down fun,
The puddles would splash, oh aren't we clever one?
So jump right in, let's not miss a beat,
In the deep well of joy, our hearts are complete!

Gentle Waves of Kindred Spirits

At the shore, where the waves meet the sand,
A crab wearing glasses struts so grand.
He says, 'Join the parade, let's dance with glee,
The ocean's our stage, come play with me!'

A dolphin named Dave jumps high in the air,
With flips and funny faces, he has no care.
He hoots and he hollers, a beach party king,
While seagulls squawk loudly, and children all sing!

With kites flying high and buckets held tight,
We splash in the sea, oh, what a delight!
The tide rolls in, making silly sounds,
As laughter and joy echo all around.

So let's ride the waves, with hearts open wide,
Sharing silly stories as time turns the tide.
For in this seaside laugh fest, let's all take part,
In gentle waves, we find laughter at heart!

Dancing in the Mist of Memories

In the morning fog, we roam,
Chasing shadows, far from home.
Laughing loud, we trip and fall,
Echoes of joy, our sweetest call.

With sticky hands and silly grins,
Splashing puddles where the fun begins.
A dance of giggles, in the haze,
Lost in the joy of silly ways.

Whispers swirl like cotton candy,
Wobbling wishes as the skies get randy.
Always waiting for the rain,
To wash away our little pain.

In each drop, a story found,
Round we go, without a sound.
Memories drip from every seam,
Dancing lightly, like a dream.

Tides of Vulnerability

The waves crash hard, they laugh and sing,
As we surf on thoughts, life's funny fling.
Fear not the tide, it's a splashy dance,
With every misstep, we take a chance.

In the sea of doubt, we ride the swell,
Float on our fears, oh can't you tell?
With jellyfish stings and a goofy grin,
We dive right in; let the fun begin!

Sandcastles crumble, but here's the jest,
We build them up, we love the mess.
Dodging the waves with hysterical fright,
It's vulnerable chaos, pure delight.

So take my hand, let's sail away,
In this tide of laughter, let's forget the gray.
With every splash that we choose to take,
We find our strength, make no mistake.

Shimmering Reflections of Devotion

Mirrored in puddles, our reflections wink,
In this fun-house world, we barely think.
With rubber duckies floating near,
We share our secrets, no need for fear.

Sometimes we trip on love's wet floor,
Creating ripples, begging for more.
Laughing like kids in a splashy play,
We find our devotion in such a way.

The sun peeks out, it starts to gleam,
Our giggles echo, a shared dream.
With raindrops twinkling, all around,
In this dance of joy, we are unbound.

So grab your towel, let's make a mess,
In the puddles of life, we are truly blessed.
For in every shimmer, every spark bright,
Lies the love we share, and it feels just right.

The Soft Lullaby of Springs

In gentle streams, we squeal with glee,
As bubbles pop, we giggle free.
With blooming flowers, we take a dip,
Sailing paper boats, on friendship's ship.

The sun smiles down, a warm embrace,
Nature's tickle, it's a funny chase.
With petals playing in the currents' song,
We wade together, where we belong.

Though frogs may croak and snails may slide,
We laugh at the bumps, it's a joyful ride.
Every splash tells tales of fun,
Under the skies, where we've just begun.

So here's to springs that sing soft tunes,
Underneath the watchful, silly moons.
Let's waddle through these watery trails,
Collecting laughter as our ship sails.

Echoes of a Bubbling Stream

Bubbles pop with glee and cheer,
Frogs croak tunes that all can hear.
Fish are dancing, quite the scene,
While ducklings waddle, oh so keen.

The water tickles all the toes,
Here comes a splash, oh, where it goes?
Rubber ducks in quite a race,
They giggle as they play their chase.

Rivers twist like contorted jokes,
Each turn spouts laughter from the folks.
The rocks just grin, they're quite a bunch,
As nature serves its Sunday brunch.

So as you stroll by, take a dip,
Join in the fun; don't take a trip!
For every splash and ripple's claim,
Is nature's way of having game.

A Symphony of Fluid Emotions

The raindrops tap a cheeky tune,
While puddles gather, singing soon.
Clouds chuckle low, a playful dance,
As sunshine joins the merry prance.

Whirlpools twirl like dancers grand,
Water winks from every hand.
Drink it in, that sweet delight,
With every sip, your heart takes flight.

Dive into the river's jest,
Where current pulls you—what a quest!
Leave your worries on the shore,
This watery jest will make you roar.

The ocean chuckles as it swells,
With salty tales and secret spells.
So paddle forth with joy abound,
In every wave, sweet laughter's found.

Cascades of Empathy

The waterfall shouts, 'Can you hear?'
Its friendly roar brings lots of cheer.
Boulders grin with mossy ties,
As splashes dance beneath the skies.

Let jellyfish sway in humor's grip,
While otters glide and do a flip.
Every ripple bears a grin,
The giggles start before they spin.

Each droplet whispers with a jest,
The streams engage in splashy fest.
Emotions flow like swirling streams,
And laughter rises through our dreams.

So take a stroll by nature's art,
Let the water tickle your heart.
In every splash, a joyful plea,
To dive right in, come splash with me!

Drenched in Heartfelt Memories

Remember when we splashed at dawn?
The garden hose became our wand.
With every spurt, we flew so high,
As rainbows formed, oh my, oh my!

The slip 'n' slide, our water ride,
With laughter mixed, we'd never hide.
Each puddle was our kingdom grand,
Where we'd splash side by side, hand in hand.

The memories drip like summer rain,
With joyous thoughts that still remain.
We played like fish; we danced like sprites,
In every splash, delight ignites.

So here today, let's honor those,
The watery days, the heartfelt prose.
With a bucket of dreams, let's fill our hearts,
For every splash is where it starts.

Heartbeats in Stillness

In a puddle, I slipped with glee,
My socks are soggy, can't you see?
A dance with droplets, what a blast,
But now I'm stuck, my fate is cast.

A garden hose turned wild and free,
Spraying neighbors, oh, what glee!
With laughter ringing through the air,
Who knew that water brought such flair?

A rubber duck sails past my nose,
Waving goodbye as it freely flows.
Splashing around, I'm quite the sight,
A water fight ignites the night.

So if you trip or take a dive,
Just laugh it off, you'll be alive!
For every splash that hits the ground,
Brings joy and giggles all around.

Lush Landscapes of Grace

A garden hose became my foe,
But what a show! Oh, what a show!
Twisting round like a snake on spree,
I swear it laughed at me, you see.

With watering cans like magic wands,
I conjured rivers with my hands.
Each flower grinned, each blade of grass,
As I became a soggy lass.

The daisies peeked beneath the rain,
And orchids teased me without restraint.
They sang a tune, I laughed along,
While worms wiggled to nature's song.

When bubbles burst in sunlight's dance,
I slipped again, oh, what a chance!
The garden's party, wild and bright,
Was worth the splashes and the fright.

Surrender to the Current

Floating down the river's bend,
I lost my shoe, but made a friend.
A fish popped up, wore a grin,
Said, 'Jump on in, let's make a spin!'

Rafts of laughter filled the stream,
With water fights, it felt like a dream.
I splashed so hard, a wave came back,
The ducks were quacking, 'What's the crack?'

The canoe tipped with a mighty 'whoosh',
And I emerged like an awkward moose.
But laughter bubbled, hearts were bright,
In currents crazy, we found delight.

With every splash and every shout,
We rode the rapids, there's no doubt.
So if you drift and find your way,
Just bob along and seize the day!

The Kiss of the Sea

Oh, salty breeze, come play with me,
I'll jump the waves, just wait and see.
But as I leap, a rogue wave roars,
And kisses me right on the shores!

Seagulls giggle as they swoop down,
With clever beaks, they'll steal my crown.
I splash my drink, the ocean's flair,
While mermaids laugh without a care.

A beach ball sails into the tide,
And I chase it like a happy guide.
But oh, that splash—a surprise today,
Now I'm soaked in seabreeze ballet!

With every wave, there's fun to find,
As water dances, intertwined.
In ocean's arms, so wild and free,
I'll be the jester of the sea!

The Sound of Water and Whispers

The raindrops dance on my shiny hat,
A symphony of giggles, and splashes, just like that.
I catch some drops in a cup, oh what fun,
My umbrella's a shield but not very well done!

A puddle calls out, a dandy little sprout,
"Jump right in, dear friend, let's twist and shout!"
The ducks quack laughter, they're ready to play,
With flippers and feathers, they brighten my day.

The river sings tunes of a slippery slide,
Where fish wear sunglasses, take joy in the ride.
I drop my shoe, it floats away free,
A fish waves goodbye, saying, "You'll miss me!"

So here's to the splashes, the dribbles and drops,
In the land of the soggy, where happiness hops.
For every little drop brings giggles galore,
In the world of wet wonders, who could ask for more?

Shores of Comfort

The beach ball bounces, we run with delight,
Sand castles crumble, oh what a sight!
Seagulls are giggling, stealing our fries,
I swear they're plotting a feast in disguise.

Waves roll in and tickle our toes,
"Watch out, here comes a big one!" everyone knows.
We jump and we splash, like kids in a race,
The ocean's our playground, a watery space.

Sun hats and sunscreen, oh what a mix,
Dad's trying to catch us, but what's the trick?
We dive and we dodge, we conquer the tide,
In our kingdom of comfort, we flounder with pride.

With shells as our treasures, we laugh and we cheer,
The shores of our laughter, we hold so dear.
For every giggle blends with the breeze,
In the realm of the silly, we do as we please!

Rivers of Hope

A river so twisty, it laughs with a cheer,
It tickles the banks, let's all gather near.
Fish flash their bonus, they're dressed to impress,
With scales so shiny, it's quite the success!

The turtles are lounging, enjoying their sun,
They giggle and wink as they pass by, so fun.
With paddles of joy, we kayak with glee,
Squeals mix with splashes, oh the jubilee!

Oh, the frogs, they croak jokes on lily pad stages,
They hold pop-up shows for all of the ages.
Each hop's a punchline, it's comedy gold,
Rivers of laughter, let the stories unfold.

So float on the current of hope and of play,
With every small ripple, we find our own way.
In the stream of our dreams, let's splash and elope,
For life's much more fun on these rivers of hope!

Circle of Life and Water

In the garden of giggles, where flowers burst forth,
The sprinklers spin round, with laughter their worth.
Kids run in circles, their shadows dance wide,
As hoses become dragons, we climb up the slide!

With buckets of joy, we splash and we sing,
The plants cheer us on, while butterflies swing.
The sun beams a smile, oh, what a sweet sight,
As rainbows appear in the warm morning light.

The squirrels throw acorns, while ducks swim in style,
In this circle of giggles, we're free for a while.
So pass me the water; it's magic, it grows,
Let's laugh 'til we fall, in this world that we know!

For life's just a circle, a splash and a giggle,
Where joy is the anchor, and laughter's a wiggle.
So hold on to fun, as the bubbles all pop,
In this circle of life, may the joy never stop!

Whispers of the Gentle Rain

Raindrops tap like laughter on the roof,
Puddles dance in joyful, silly proof.
Umbrellas twirl like hats on a whim,
Dancing through drops, we're splashed to the brim.

The clouds wear frowns, but they're just pretending,
Their tears are jokes, not a sad ending.
Giggles drip down from the playful sky,
As we run in circles, you and I.

Each splash a story, each giggle a song,
In this splash zone, we feel we belong.
The ground below's a trampoline made,
With every jump, our worries do fade.

So let it rain, let the heavens applaud,
For each droplet's a cheer from the sod.
Let's paint with puddles, you're my best friend,
In this watery world, the fun never ends.

Embracing the Cascade of Hearts

A river flows, wiggling like a worm,
With tales of love at every curve and turn.
It spills out secrets, mischievous glee,
Where fish wear glasses, as you can see!

Boulders chuckle under a wave's sweet kiss,
Riding the currents, what's not to miss?
The ducks debate over who swam best,
While frogs hold a concert—there's no time to rest.

To splash, to laugh, is the river's appeal,
As we wade in deep, it's like a big meal.
Full of good humor, a festival bright,
Cascading love, oh, what a delight!

So gather your friends for a splashy parade,
With giggles and bubbles that never will fade.
These waters of fun, they're meant to share,
In the embrace of joy, there's love everywhere.

Beneath the Surface of Affection

Bubbles rise up with squeaks and a pop,
An ocean of joy, we'll never stop.
With seaweed hair and fishy attire,
We dance underwater, our hearts on fire.

The clams giggle, shells clapping in tune,
As we twirl past the starfish beneath the moon.
A turtle wearing shades, how cool is that?
In this underwater world, we roam like a cat.

Mermaids tell tales of glitter and dreams,
While dolphins explore in hilarious teams.
With laughter as deep as the ocean's own floor,
We float through the waves wanting nothing more.

So dive with me down where the fun never ends,
We'll splash through the bubbles, just love and good friends.
In this current of joy, we'll wiggle and sway,
Beneath the surface, let's laugh all day!

Rivers Flowing with Tenderness

A stream flows gently with a grin on its face,
Tickling the rocks in a playful embrace.
With each gentle splash, a giggle is born,
As flowers throw petals, all bright and adorned.

The fish wear bow ties, oh what a sight,
Trying to dance in the shimmering light.
They nudge and they joke as we sit on the bank,
Splashing around while our hearts fill their tank.

A mossy old log's the perfect stage,
As critters perform in this wet little cage.
They take a deep bow, then leap and they play,
In the rippling waters, we're lost in the sway.

So gather 'round friends for a river's delight,
We'll toast with the frogs in the soft moonlight.
The currents of joy will forever be ours,
As we swirl with the giggles beneath twinkling stars.

The Vitality of Fluid Bonds

In the glass, a little splash,
A sip that makes us laugh and dash,
Wobbling cups and soggy floors,
Who knew love could spill from doors?

When kids play tag with drippy hoses,
And neighbors laugh at muddy poses,
We dance around the puddles wide,
In liquid joy, our hearts abide.

An umbrella flips, a raincoat's fight,
While splashes of joy take off in flight,
The more we splash, the more we bond,
In silly swims, we go beyond.

So let's not fuss about the mess,
For in each drop, there's pure success,
With fluid grace, we'll always find,
That laughter flows and joy's entwined.

Under the Bridge of Care

Beneath the bridge, we dangle feet,
In muddy waters, life feels sweet,
With rubber ducks that squeak so loud,
Our laughter echoes, we're love-proud.

The river sings a giddy tune,
As frogs croak in a silly swoon,
Splashing friends and giggly fish,
A wish to grant that muddy bliss.

Our snacks float by on cute little rafts,
While we weave dreams with silly crafts,
Under the sun, a playful spark,
A splash of joy ignites the dark.

Forget the rules, let's have a ball,
With every wave, we just might fall,
Yet, in this flood of cheeky cheer,
We bridge our hearts, let's give a cheer!

Whimsy in the Water

In puddles deep, we jump and play,
Our rubber boots are bold today,
With each wet squish, we giggle loud,
Creating chaos, we're supremely proud.

The hose gets turned, oh what a spray,
Sending giggles soaring away,
Wet hair, wild and full of fun,
In soft showers, our hearts outrun.

Floating paper boats, a grand parade,
With every wave, a new escapade,
The sun shines bright, our spirits soar,
In laughter's tide, we ask for more.

So raise a glass to playful tides,
We'll ride the waves wherever it glides,
In whimsy's flow, our hearts entwined,
Together in joy, the best we find.

Love's Gentle Hum

A cup of tea, we sip and grin,
With silly chats, where to begin?
We spill the beans, the milk takes flight,
In tender moments, everything's right.

The drips from rain, a playful song,
As giggles echo, they can't be wrong,
We chase the clouds, we dance with dreams,
In the sweet chaos, our laughter beams.

A splash of cheer, a tickle fight,
We're soaked in joy, it feels so right,
The water bonds us, silly and true,
In every drop, I cherish you.

So let the currents flow and tease,
In gentle hums, we find our ease,
With every laugh, my heart will drum,
In playful waves, love's gentle hum.

Rivulet Reflections

Little streams giggle with glee,
Splashes of joy dance carefree.
Frogs in tuxedos, ready to leap,
Ripples of laughter, secrets to keep.

Drifting leaves, a comedic sight,
Dancing in circles, pure delight.
A fish with a bowtie joins the fun,
Winking at ducks, oh what a pun!

Silly clouds drift overhead,
Whispering jokes, twice they've said.
The sun chuckles, a bright yellow grin,
Join the splash, let the giggles begin!

In puddles, reflections make us smile,
Wiggly worms waltz, tease us a while.
Nature's circus, a merry show,
With each tiny splash, our spirits grow.

Sailing on Serenity

On calm waves, we drift about,
With seagulls chirping, no doubt.
A boat with a hat sails by so grand,
While waves make jokes, oh isn't it bland?

Clouds are comedians in the sky,
Throwing rain jokes that make us cry.
The tide has rhythm, a playful beat,
As laughter echoes from every seat.

Sunbeams peek in, a peek-a-boo,
Stealing the spotlight, they shine right through.
Splashing along, we tickle the sea,
Sailing on laughter, just you and me.

With salt on our smiles, we float along,
Creating our world, where we belong.
As waves sing softly, we join their tune,
Adventurous hearts underneath the moon.

The Pool of Warmth

In the pool of fun, laughter does splash,
Rubber ducks dance in a bubbly bash.
Kids with giggles, the stars of the show,
Making big waves wherever they go.

Floaties in shades, all wearing a frown,
Refusing to sink, they're kings of this town.
The water tickles, we squeal in delight,
Whimsical ripples come out for a fight.

The sun's a lifeguard, with shades on his face,
Blowing a whistle, keeping up the pace.
Each splash is a story, each giggle a rhyme,
In the pool of warmth, we lose track of time.

When the sun sets low, and dusk takes the stage,
We still play on, carefree and un-caged.
Here's to the splashes, the laughter and cheer,
In our pool of warmth, there's nothing to fear.

Streams of Acceptance

In a flowing river, where quirks intertwine,
Fish wear bow ties, sipping sunshine.
The beavers build castles like kings on the stream,
While turtles float by, living the dream.

The water-will spins, a swirling delight,
Churning up silliness by day and by night.
An otter throws parties, what a wild spree,
Jumping in joy, the life of the sea.

A duck with a monocle leads the parade,
Spreading acceptance, no need to be afraid.
Waves chuckle softly, as they roll past the shore,
Embracing each splash, always wanting more.

Love flows like water, it's funny and free,
In streams of acceptance, we're meant to be.
So take my hand, let's leap in alive,
In this hilarious world, we thrive and dive!

Wells of Warmth and Trust

In a well so deep and wide,
I dropped my heart, it took a ride.
It splashed around, it did a twirl,
and came back up, my love to whirl.

We tossed our fears into the well,
danced around, what a funny spell!
Laughter echoed, ripples grew,
who knew a joke could flow like dew?

A fish jumped out, a winked surprise,
it cracked a joke, oh what a guise!
We giggled loud, the water swayed,
as trust was built, unafraid.

So here we are, with hearts all bright,
a silly splash in love's delight.
In the wells of warmth and cheer,
you'll find me, dear, come sit right here.

Embracing the Storm

When clouds rolled in with thunder's roar,
we built a boat—who could ask for more?
Paddles splashed, our laughter soared,
in stormy seas, we swiftly floored.

Umbrellas flew like jellyfish,
a windblown kiss—a funny wish!
The waves crashed high, we danced anew,
as rain became our playful brew.

We caught a wave, we rode so free,
yelling out, "Look at me!"
With every splash, a giggle shared,
what fun we had, nothing compared.

So here we float, in laughter's stream,
giddy hearts, we dare to dream.
In stormy times, we find our glee,
you and I, just you and me.

The Flow of Gentle Words

A river spoke in whispers light,
like butterflies that danced in flight.
Each word a ripple, soft and sweet,
a humor twist in every beat.

We sat by banks, exchanging jokes,
as giggles bubbled—just old folks!
The water flowed, but oh, how fun,
the stories spun, we came undone.

A fish swam by with a cheeky grin,
it winked at us, we laughed within.
Our gentle words made currents sway,
who knew that friendship could play this way?

So let them flow, our witty quips,
like rivers run with playful dips.
In every line, a laugh transcends,
the flow of words, where joy descends.

Cradled in the Ocean's Embrace

The ocean rocked us, waves so wide,
in salty hugs, we laughed and cried.
Seashells whispered secrets sweet,
a treasure hunt beneath our feet.

With every splash, a giddy cheer,
the water tickled, drew us near.
A crab danced on, a funny sight,
under the sun, our hearts took flight.

We built sandcastles, towers high,
holding on to dreams that could fly.
And when they fell, we laughed out loud,
in ocean's swells, we felt so proud.

So here we are, in nature's play,
in waves that rock us night and day.
Cradled in joy, let laughter spring,
in ocean's arms, our hearts take wing.

In the Garden of Embrace

In a garden so lush, so green and bright,
A gnome on a swing, what a silly sight!
With plants in hats, and flowers that dance,
They giggle and prance, it's a whimsical chance.

Bees buzzing tunes, a waltz in the air,
They twirl with the daisies, without a care.
A watering can spills, but oh what a mess,
The earth starts to chuckle, it's anyone's guess!

A carrot in socks, what a sight to behold,
It shimmies and shakes, so brave and bold.
With laughter like rain, humor does flow,
In this garden of joy, love's seeds overflow.

So gather your friends, let's dance and play,
In our patch of delight, we'll splash all day!
With giggles and grins, it's a riot, you see,
In the garden of sunshine, we all feel so free!

Raindrop Serenade

Pitter-patter raindrops on the roof above,
Playing music of joy, a splashy love.
Each droplet a dancer, twirling with flair,
A puddle party forms, splashing everywhere!

The umbrellas parade, all colors so bright,
Silly hats bounce, oh what a sight!
Jumping in puddles, we stomp and we squish,
Chasing each other, just making a wish.

With laughter like bubbles, we float to the sky,
As raindrops come down, none ask us why.
We laugh till we're soggy, then laugh some more,
In a symphony wet, where we all adore!

So dance in the rain, let your cares wash away,
A giggle brigade making rainy days play.
With splashes and grins, together we sing,
In this raindrop serenade, let the joy ring!

Cascades of Kindness

A fountain of laughter in the park we run,
Where kindness flows freely, oh what fun!
With big splashes of joy and small jokes around,
Each giggle a ripple, oh how they abound!

Splashing through puddles, a slip and a slide,
We giggle together, can't hide how we cried.
Like fountains of sweetness, all gushing with cheer,
Grinning like dolphins, we're all feeling queer!

A water balloon toss, oh what a delight,
Flying through the air, not a target in sight!
Onlookers just laugh as we burst with a roar,
In cascades of kindness, we want to explore!

So gather your pals, let the laughter flow,
In this wacky wonderland, let's steal the show.
With splashes of joy and a kind-hearted aim,
In these cascades of laughter, we ignite the flame!

Love's Liquid Embrace

In a teacup pond, where the goldfish dance,
Frog jumps in sideways, giving romance a chance.
With splashes of giggles, they swirl round and round,
Creating ripples of joy that echo the sound.

A watering hose sings a quirky old song,
While critters all shuffle, it's merry and strong.
With wildflowers as capes, they twirl and they spin,
A parade of the silly, with laughter within!

Fingers dipped gently in water so cool,
We splash each other playfully, breaking the rule.
The garden's alive, with a humorous twist,
As petals take flight, waving goodbye to the mist.

So let's toast with cups of lemonade bright,
To the joyful moments that feel just so right.
With every sip taken, love bubbles with ease,
In love's liquid laughter, our hearts find their peace!

Pools of Serenity and Affection

In a pool of giggles we dive,
Splashing joy, oh, we're alive!
Rubber ducks float with glee,
In this watery spree, just you and me.

The sunbeams dance on our heads,
Like playful fish jumping from beds.
Laughter echoes, bubbles rise,
In our little world, joy never dies.

Around we swirl, we spin and glide,
Our hearts, like water, open wide.
With every splash, a silly grin,
In this pool, we find love within.

So grab a float, let's ride the tide,
In this laughter, we'll always abide.
Each wave of joy comes to play,
Drenched in giggles, come what may.

The Essence of Love in Every Wave

Each wave that rolls, a hug from the sea,
With seaweed tickles, oh, what glee!
As we surf the swell with style,
Every splash makes us laugh for a while.

Saltwater kisses on our cheeks,
Giggles echo as the ocean speaks.
Jumping in as the tide pulls back,
Every wave brings joy, never lack.

Crabs dance sideways, what a sight,
Trying to join our silly fight.
With seashells ringing like little bells,
We discover love in our ocean spells.

So come on, splash, and lose our fears,
Our hearts float high in salty tears.
Each wave a wink, each rush a tease,
In this watery fun, we find our ease.

Raindrops on the Canvas of Life

Raindrops tap, a playful beat,
Filling puddles beneath our feet.
We jump and shout, a splash explosion,
Creating joy, a wet devotion.

Each droplet sings a silly tune,
Bouncing off the ground, we swoon.
Umbrellas turn into funny hats,
As we dance with whimsical splats.

The cloudy sky's our canvas bright,
With colors splashed in sheer delight.
We paint our laughter in rainy streams,
Crafting tales from puddly dreams.

So let it rain, we'll spin and shout,
Nature's giggles, there's no doubt.
Every droplet is a playful poke,
Life's a joke, and we're the joke.

Shallows of Shared Dreams

In the shallows where we play,
Water hugs us, come what may.
We'll build sandcastles, oh so tall,
Just to watch them wobble and fall.

With each footprint, we leave a mark,
Silly stories, our own spark.
Starfish giggle, shells all grin,
In this shallow, we both win.

Riding waves on inflatable steeds,
Our laughter grows like ocean weeds.
We splash like dolphins, joy so wide,
In this shallow, love's our guide.

So let's explore the sandy shore,
Each wave brings new fun, explore more!
In these shallows, dreams take flight,
With every giggle, the world feels right.

Dewdrops of Desire

Dewdrops dance on leaves so bright,
Tickling petals in morning light.
Bees buzz loudly, sipping delight,
As laughter bubbles, taking flight.

Raining jokes from skies so clear,
Puddles splash with uncontained cheer.
A sunflower wiggles, oh dear,
Wants to join in, it's quite sincere.

Worms in the soil chuckle below,
Giggling at plants putting on a show.
Nature's antics, go with the flow,
In this garden, love will grow.

Frogs in a chorus, croaking so loud,
Bouncing to rhythms, feeling quite proud.
With every drop, they gather a crowd,
Who knew being green could be so endowed?

Floating on Affection

In a puddle, ducks quack and glide,
Waddling wildly, they're filled with pride.
Their splashy dance, too funny to hide,
While the grumpy old cat just sighed.

Clouds float by, like marshmallows sweet,
Daring each other to compete.
They bump and tumble, a fluffy treat,
While the sun smirks, enjoying the feat.

Raindrops gather on windowpanes,
Sliding down like racing trains.
They giggle and cheer, ignoring the rains,
Singing love songs, breaking all chains.

In a boat made of love's own design,
Sailing in circles, feeling divine.
Every wave carries laughter, a sign,
That affection's the best, you can't confine!

Wellspring of Support

Bubbles burst, making rather loud sounds,
As friends dive in with splashes abound.
Cheerful whispers echo around,
In this well, love and laughter are found.

Throw in a coin, wish for a laugh,
Jokes sink down and make quite a mess.
With each ripple, they start a new path,
Overflowing joy, nobody's distressed.

Fish in tuxedos swim by with flair,
Dancing to tunes, without a care.
An octopus juggles, oh what a pair,
Support is tight, it's love we all share.

Splash fights erupt, dodging the spray,
In this wellspring, we play all day.
United in giggles, come what may,
Love's buoyant nature, leading the way!

Under the Canopy of Care

Under the branches, laughing so free,
Squirrels compete in playful glee.
Dropping acorns, they climb a tree,
Sharing stories of wiggly spaghetti!

Raindrops play, tapping on the leaf,
Every plop brings a moment of relief.
With dancing shadows, there's never grief,
A canopy of joy, beyond belief.

Fluffy clouds look down, giggling with pride,
As the sun peeks in, a ray to guide.
Butterflies twirl, with charm they abide,
In this realm, all sorrows subside.

Wrap in the warmth of a cozy embrace,
Nature's love song fills every space.
With laughter and cheer, there's no better place,
Under this canopy, life's a joyful race!

Chasing Waterfalls of Joy

In the park we play, oh what a sight,
Splashing in puddles, laughter so bright.
Kites fly high, like ducks in a race,
Chasing joy's rivers, with smiles on our face.

The squirrels all giggle, their cheeks full of nuts,
As we skip through the streams and puddles like muts.
Who knew that a splash could cause such delight?
A sunny day's magic, oh what a bite!

Fetch me the hose, let's create a wave,
Water fights break out, it's fun that we crave.
You dodge and you weave, but I'm always right here,
Drenched in our laughter, no reason to sneer.

Under rainbows we dance, no need to be shy,
The world is our playground, just you and I.
So let's embrace play, let's run and not stop,
In this waterfall dream, we'll laugh till we drop.

Enveloped by the Stream

In a small little creek, where the fish laugh away,
We toss in some pebbles, what a delightful fray.
Frogs croak a tune, as they leap through the air,
We giggle and grin, without any care.

Hiding behind bushes, we throw silly tricks,
Splashing our friends, oh what a mix!
"Fishy, come dance!" we joyfully sing,
As the water gives hugs and the ripples just swing.

The turtles all gossip, in their slow little shells,
While we catch them giggling, spinning their tales.
Crazy adventures, jumping rain clouds above,
Playing in streams is a splash of pure love.

Every splash, every chill, we rise with a grin,
Life's just a game when you dive right in.
So let's fill our hearts with this wonderful spree,
In our stream of giggles, just you, and just me.

Echoes of Rain and Love

Raindrops are drummers on my window pane,
Little beats of laughter, echo with no pain.
Dancing like kittens, splashes galore,
Each puddle a dancefloor, oh who could ask for more?

Umbrella turned inside, it's a hat for the bold,
We twirl in the rain, laughter never gets old.
With each little raindrop, a tickle and tease,
Our hearts shine bright, like a stormy breeze.

Can you hear the clouds? They're cracking up too,
As the sky chuckles down, like a friend so true.
With splashes of mirth and puddles of fun,
We'll frolic till we're old, and the rain's all done.

So let's skip through the thunder, dance in delight,
Raindrops keep telling us, everything's alright.
In this echo of joy that drizzles above,
We'll laugh through the storms, in the showers of love.

Beneath the Surface Lies Trust

Deep in the pond, where the goldfish parade,
We gather our dreams in a grand charade.
With swirls of bright colors and splashes of cheer,
We ignore all the worries, just let's persevere.

The ducks are our judges, quacking away,
As we dive and we wiggle, in silly display.
Holding our breath, we play hide and seek,
Trusting the bubbles, no need to be meek.

Oh, what a treasure beneath all that green,
The secrets we whisper, the laughs that we glean.
With each little ripple that bounces up high,
We find our reflections, just you and I.

So let's jump in together, let's make quite a fuss,
Life is much sweeter, beneath that trust.
In waters of giggles, we'll surf on this wave,
Where joy is the current, and laughter we crave.

Drifting into Affection

In a puddle I saw a duck,
Waddling past, oh what luck!
He quacked a tune, a silly song,
Splashing around, where I belong.

My heart did float on this sweet ride,
With every splash, love swelled inside.
The sun peeked out, a grin so wide,
We danced together, side by side.

Coffee spilled, it rained on my shirt,
I laughed loudly, life's a flirty flirt.
With every drop, a giggle we share,
In this watery love, floating with flair.

So let's drift on this playful sea,
Full of laughter, just you and me.
No need for boats, just hugs and sighs,
In this puddled joy, our spirits rise.

A Symphony of Reflections

A teapot sings, it starts to whistle,
I swear it's dancing, or maybe a missile.
Tea spills over, oh what a sight,
I'm not mad, it's pure delight!

Bubbles form, a bubbly chorus,
Each one pops, love's uproarious.
The washcloth joins, in a soft whirl,
In this kitchen, my heart starts to twirl.

The sink's a stage, as dishes leap,
Dancing forks, oh, how they creep!
With every clink, a sweet serenade,
Turn up the tunes, let worries fade.

So grab a cup, take a sip so bright,
It's a splashy concert, a sheer delight.
With every note, affection hums,
Life's a melody, and fun becomes.

The Fragrance of Rain

Raindrops fall, a drumming beat,
Wet shoes squish, oh what a treat!
I leap in puddles, a splashy kick,
With every jump, I get more slick.

The clouds above wear a frown so gray,
But I dance beneath, come what may.
Umbrellas float like sails on high,
With each gust, my laughter will fly.

Rain boots squelch, a squishy tune,
Every splatter's a laugh, oh so attune.
I'll twirl and spin in this drizzly dance,
In the fragrance of rain, challenge all chance.

So let it pour, let laughter reign,
Every drop a chuckle, no room for pain.
Through puddles of joy, I happily roam,
In this loving downpour, I feel at home.

Echoes of the Tides

The ocean waves, they roll and play,
Whispering secrets, drifting away.
Shells come in, with silly faces,
Talking trash, in funny places.

Seagulls squawk, they steal my fries,
With those antics, how can I despise?
Each wave brings a chuckle, so divine,
As I dance on sand, feeling fine.

The tide pulls back, a great surprise,
With every wave, my giggle flies.
Splashing around, like a bubbly sprite,
In saltwater laughter, everything feels right.

So let's embrace these coastlines wide,
In ocean whispers, our hearts collide.
Each wave a joke, done with glee,
In every echo, love flows free.

www.ingramcontent.com/pod-product-compliance
Lightning Source LLC
Chambersburg PA
CBHW070310120526
44590CB00017B/2620